Railwa
Central Scotland
2016–20

IAN LOTHIAN

BRITAIN'S RAILWAYS SERIES, VOLUME 14

Front cover image: 43149 leads the 11.39 from Glasgow Queen Street to Aberdeen at Bardrill, between Blackford and Gleneagles, with 43035 the trailing power car on 20 September 2019.

Back cover image: 66746 leads the *Royal Scotsman* at Craigenhill on 16 September 2016 on its way from Edinburgh to Arrochar and Tarbert with 66743 on the rear.

Contents page image: On 24 February 2017, 60002 passes Bardrill, between Blackford and Gleneagles, with the 05.55 Oxwellmains to Aberdeen cement.

Published by Key Books
An imprint of Key Publishing Ltd
PO Box 100
Stamford
Lincs PE19 1XQ

www.keypublishing.com

The right of Ian Lothian to be identified as the author of this book has been asserted in accordance with the Copyright, Designs and Patents Act 1988 Sections 77 and 78.

Typeset by SJmagic DESIGN SERVICES, India.

Contents

Introduction

The five-year period covered by this book saw a vast number of changes to the rail network in Central Scotland; so much so that it was not a simple task of which illustrations to include but more a case of which ones would have to be left out due to space limitations.

By the end of 2020, the rail network was very different from how it was in January 2016; a programme of electrification has resulted in there now being five electrified routes between Edinburgh and Glasgow, Central Scotland's two largest cities. The five are Glasgow Central to Edinburgh Waverley via Carstairs, Glasgow Central to Edinburgh Waverley via Shotts, Glasgow Queen Street Low Level to Edinburgh Waverley via Airdrie and Bathgate, Glasgow Queen Street to Edinburgh Waverley via Cumbernauld and Falkirk Grahamston and the flagship route of Queen Street to Waverley via Falkirk High.

ScotRail services on the Carstairs line are usually worked by Class 380 EMUs; the Queen Street Low Level to Edinburgh line is the preserve of the Class 334 EMUs while the Shotts services are mainly Class 385 with the occasional service producing a Class 380. The Queen Street to Waverley services by both the lines through Falkirk Grahamston and Falkirk High are worked by the Hitachi-built Class 385 EMUs. To offer increased capacity on the route via Falkirk High, some platforms at Queen Street station were lengthened to accommodate eight-coach trains, and the station was given a new frontage while a new platform was also constructed at Edinburgh Waverley.

ScotRail's inter-city services are now worked by a mix of Class 170 DMUs and refurbished HSTs, while the LNER HSTs have in turn been displaced by bi-mode Hitachi Azumas. Virgin West Coast lost the franchise and West Coast services are now operated by Avanti. TransPennine Express services to both Edinburgh and Glasgow are now worked by new trains, those to and from Manchester Airport utilise CAF-built five-car Class 397 EMUs while the franchise's East Coast services between Edinburgh Waverley and Liverpool Lime Street are operated by five-car Hitachi Class 802 bi-modes. To complete the new passenger stock line-up, Caledonian Sleeper has introduced new Mark 5 coaches, these also coming from the CAF plant in Spain.

On the freight side, Colas Railfreight took delivery of more General Electric Class 70 locomotives built in Erie, Pennsylvania, and these are now to be found on oil trains out of Grangemouth and the cement trains from Oxwellmains. Freightliner took delivery late in 2020 of more Class 90 locomotives that had been displaced from passenger duties in East Anglia while DRS introduced new Class 88 bi-mode locomotives.

Changes have occurred in almost every operational area and trying to record this has not been an easy task. I must state that the illustrations used are how I have recorded the changes; others could have interpreted events differently but the contents of this book are how I have seen things evolve.

A case of having to expect the unexpected was the emergence of the Covid-19 pandemic in 2020 with the imposition of a lockdown, with people being urged to work from home and to avoid using public transport. The number of passengers carried on the railways of Central Scotland dropped dramatically and the frequency of train services on some lines was reduced. With the pandemic still raging at the beginning of 2021 when this book was written, the long term effects on passenger services is unclear.

I could never have managed to be out with my camera and be in the right place at the right time without the help and assistance of so many who have kindly told me what, where and when certain events would be happening. That would be a long list but to you all I have to offer a very big thank you. My thanks go to all at Key Publishing who have helped me to produce this book; something I had always wanted to do and now have managed. Lastly, but by no means least, I have to acknowledge the help and encouragement given to me by my two children, Chris and Laura, and above all the help and support given to me at all times by my wife Irene, as without her assistance it would not have been possible for me to produce this book.

66428 approaches Larbert on 6 May 2020 with the 13.07 Stobart/Tesco intermodal from Inverness to Mossend.

Chapter 1

Lines to Carstairs and on to Glasgow Central

The words that can sum up the happenings during these five years would be 'It was a time of great change'. In 2016, Virgin Trains operated its West Coast services to Birmingham and London using a fleet of Class 390 tilting Pendolinos. The company's red and silver colours were well known as Virgin had operated these services since 9 March 1997 but all this was about to change. When the West Coast franchise came up for renewal, Virgin was disbarred from the bidding process and the franchise was awarded to Avanti, a company owned by First Group and the Italian transport firm Trenitalia. The first sign of the change to come was when the Pendolinos went for maintenance that included a repaint and emerged in an all-over white. After Avanti took over on 7 December 2019, the end coaches in a Class 390 set started to appear in a new green livery, almost the complete opposite of the former red and silver.

TransPennine Express operates the services between Edinburgh and Glasgow to Manchester Airport and in 2020, a new service between Glasgow Central and Liverpool Lime Street was introduced. In 2016, the services were operated by a fleet of ten four-car Class 350/4 EMUs built between 2013 and 2014 by Siemens at Krefeld in Germany. From the autumn of 2019, these units were gradually replaced by 12 five-car Class 397 'Civity' EMUs built by CAF in Spain and the Class 350/4s were transferred to West Midlands Trains.

CrossCountry was the only passenger franchise that during the five years covered by this book continued to operate on the same routes using the same stock, this being a mix of a small fleet of HSTs and the Class 220 and 221 Voyagers.

ScotRail services between Edinburgh Waverley and Glasgow Central via Carstairs were mainly operated by the Class 380 EMUs but on the suburban services to Lanark that use the WCML, the big change was the introduction of the Hitachi-built Class 385 EMUs. ScotRail also acquired 12 four-car Class 321 EMUs from London Midland and, after removing one coach, they were renumbered as Class 320/4s so that they were identical to the ScotRail-operated 1990-built Class 320/3s.

The introduction of the Class 385s allowed stock previously used on Lanark services to be cascaded to other routes and also for all of the Class 314 EMUs to be withdrawn from service at the end of 2019. Caledonian Sleeper also went through a major change with new Mark 5 coaches built by CAF in Spain and using Class 92 locomotives for haulage between London Euston and Edinburgh and Glasgow.

Freight services changed with an increase in the number of intermodal container services from a variety of locations serving several destinations within Central Scotland. The big change was the end of the once substantial number of coal trains that had been running and this is illustrated by the image of the former coal loading plant at Ravenstruther being demolished in early 2016 following the collapse of Scottish Coal and the closure of its opencast mining sites in the Douglas Basin, the coal from there having at one time been transported by road to Ravenstruther.

Not to be outdone by the introduction of new passenger rolling stock, the freight sector also saw the introduction of new motive power. Colas Railfreight introduced new Class 70 locomotives, built in Erie, Pennsylvania, and they started to appear on the Grangemouth to Dalston fuel tanks as well as the Aberdeen to Workington Docks calcium carbonate tanks. Direct Rail Services (DRS) introduced ten Class 88 bi-mode locomotives, principally electric but with a small diesel engine that was capable of moving a train in and out of sidings at freight terminals where there were no overhead wires. These locomotives are now the regular power on the Stobart/Tesco intermodal services between Daventry and Mossend, except that during the leaf fall period, the trains have to be double-headed because of the type's light weight. The second locomotive ensures that any wheel-slipping over Shap and Beattock can be overcome, allowing timings to be maintained and no delays caused to other services.

There have always been changes to the railway scene but the number of alterations that have occurred in such a short period of time involving so many types of trains and their liveries during the five years from 2016 to the end of 2020 has really been unprecedented.

On a bitterly cold 28 December 2017, 60047 leaves the Border hills behind at Pettinain as it approaches Carstairs with the 08.25 Dalston to Grangemouth empty fuel tanks.

In some very welcome late autumn sunshine, 66741 is nearing Carstairs on 2 November 2017 with the 12.16 Carlisle to Millerhill infrastructure service.

88007 has just crossed Float Viaduct over the River Clyde, just to the south of Carstairs, with the Sunday afternoon Mossend to Daventry Tesco intermodal on 25 February 2018.

390151 is heading south on the West Coast Main Line at Float Viaduct on 25 February 2018 with the 14.51 Edinburgh Waverley to Euston via Birmingham. 390151 is adorned with the Virgin Trains 'Business is Great Britain' logo and the Union Flag at each end.

An unidentified TransPennine Express Class 350/4 was approaching Float Viaduct on 2 November 2017 while working the 12.00 service from Manchester Airport to Edinburgh Waverley.

By the spring of 2020, the Class 350 EMUs had been replaced on TransPennine services by the new Class 397s, built by CAF in Spain. On 31 July 2020, 397009 is seen passing Auchengray with the 08.12 from Edinburgh Waverley to Manchester Airport.

With a full load of 28 containers behind it, 66221 runs downgrade at Auchengray on 27 January 2017 with the 04.22 from Tees Dock to Mossend.

68011 in its Chiltern Railways livery was an unusual visitor to Scotland on 10 May 2016, seen as it passes Auchengray with two nuclear flasks from Torness to Sellafield with 37604 on the rear.

The empty stock from the overnight Caledonian Sleeper from London to Edinburgh is always taken from Edinburgh to Polmadie depot in Glasgow for cleaning and servicing. On 31 July 2020, the 08.19 from Waverley to Polmadie is seen as it passes Auchengray with GBRf-liveried 92043 hauling the train instead of the usual Caledonian Sleeper-liveried Class 92.

Following the collapse of Scottish Coal and the lack of demand for coal as a fuel for power stations, the former coal loading plant at Ravenstruther, which used to generate several loaded coal trains every day, was being demolished on 7 March 2016.

On 23 November 2016, Freightliner's 66562 powers north on the WCML at Ravenstruther with the 05.06 intermodal from Daventry to Coatbridge, a seasonal service that normally only ran for about two months prior to Christmas every year.

A freight service that has seen many changes to its haulage is the 06.16 Daventry to Mossend Tesco Intermodal. On 24 August 2016, the train is seen as it passes Ravenstruther behind a pair of DRS Class 68s with 68018 leading 68021.

Virgin Trains had operated West Coast services for many years but had lost the franchise. As a result, when a class 390 went through maintenance, the Virgin branding was removed and the set emerged in this all-over white livery. On 10 January 2020, 390152 passed Ravenstruther while working the 07.15 from Birmingham New Street to Glasgow Central.

Colas Railfreight had ordered more Class 70 locomotives from General Electric in the USA. The 3,820hp locos were constructed at Erie, Pennsylvania, and one of the new batch that was delivered in 2017, 70811 was in charge of the 08.25 Dalston to Grangemouth empty fuel tanks on 8 December 2017, seen as it passed Ravenstruther.

A pair of the Royal Mail Class 325 EMUs speed south on the WCML at Ravenstruther on 25 November 2016 with the 12.34 Shieldmuir to Warrington at the start of additional mail services for the weeks prior to Christmas.

DRS took delivery of ten Class 88 electric locomotives between 2015 and 2016. The 5,360hp locomotives were built by Vossloh/ Stadler at Valencia in Spain. To make sure that there were no adhesion problems with any adverse rail conditions caused by leaf-fall, the northbound train on 2 November 2017 was double-headed by 88006 and 88003, seen as they crested Craigenhill Summit and started the descent towards Carluke.

Pendolino 390044 passes Craigenhill on 19 November 2020 while working the 09.10 from London Euston to Glasgow Central. The two end cars have received the colours of the new operator, Avanti, while the coaches still remain in unbranded white.

68007 was one of two DRS Class 68s turned out in ScotRail Saltire livery for working morning and evening commuter services between Fife and Edinburgh. On 21 January 2017, 68007 was caught by my camera as it passed Craigenhill taking container flats from Craigentinny to Motherwell. The wagons had been at Craigentinny for tyre turning on the depot's wheel lathe.

A pair of ScotRail's new Class 385/0s, 385003 and 385001, pass Cartland on 18 September 2020 with the 11.16 from Glasgow Central to Lanark, a new duty for this class.

One of the new TransPennine Class 397s, 397009, was working the 12.03 from Glasgow Central to Liverpool Lime Street at Cartland on 18 September 2020, a new service that only commenced with the latest franchise.

66164 was making a fairly slow but steady climb up to Craigenhill Summit when it passed Cartland on 25 September 2020 with a fully laden 08.24 Mossend to Tees Dock. While many other types of freight have shrunk, intermodal container traffic is one that continues to grow.

380111 has stopped at Motherwell for a crew change while working an Edinburgh Waverley to Ayr via Glasgow Central ScotRail service on 4 June 2016.

320416 and 320313 arrive at Motherwell on 4 June 2016 with a Cumbernauld to Anderston service. 320416 was still in its London Midland colours, having just been acquired by ScotRail and renumbered and shortened from a four-car Class 321 to a three-car Class 320. Within a matter of days, it was sent for repainting into ScotRail Saltire livery.

In their last full year of service, 314210 and 314214 are seen on the approaches to Glasgow Central; 314210 on a service from Neilston while 314214 has just departed for Wemyss Bay on 21 September 2018.

While Glasgow Queen Street was closed in early 2016 for engineering work for the forthcoming electrification of the main line to Edinburgh via Falkirk High, services between Glasgow and Aberdeen were diverted to Glasgow Central. On 22 March 2016, 170415 waits at Central with a service to Aberdeen while 221102 is just about to depart with the 10.00 to London Euston via Birmingham New Street.

Chapter 2
In and Around Glasgow

The theme of change is one that continues with this look at the rail scene around Glasgow. In December 2016, I travelled to Shields Road depot to see the official launch of the new Hitachi-built Class 385 EMUs. The build programme of these units was running late and although 385102 looked impressive under the lights, all was not what it seemed. The unit was devoid of any interior fittings but was wired up to numerous computers for when the unit was to be tested on the main lines. The initial line chosen for testing was that to Wemyss Bay during the night when there were no other trains on the line. After the completion of the overnight test run, the unit was pulled to Gourock where it was stabled during the day. The unit was hauled to and from Gourock by DB Class 66s, which is why 66115 can be seen in this chapter, as it had hauled 385102 back to Gourock after the previous night's tests.

The middle line that was laid between Shields Junction and the outskirts of Paisley is now fully used by ScotRail passenger services and with bi-directional signalling, it has proved to be a very useful addition to the network. The lines from Glasgow Central to East Kilbride and Barrhead are the next two suburban lines scheduled for electrification with parts of the East Kilbride line also set to see a second track laid where it is at present only single track. Improvements will also be made to stations and signalling. A few years ago, Glasgow Central was criticised for having poor air quality due to the number of diesel trains working out of the station so removing more DMUs will further help to improve this situation.

Other improvements to the suburban network saw the platforms at Milngavie lengthened so that they could accommodate nine coaches in length, meaning that a three-car unit could be stabled at the bufferstops while a six-coach set could arrive and have the necessary platform room. This project was completed just before the end of 2020, and it had also resulted in alterations to the track, signalling and the overhead power lines.

A new station was constructed and opened at Robroyston, on the line between Springburn and Stepps, to serve an area where a substantial number of new houses are to be built. The station also has a large car park that is next to the M80 motorway and will also serve as a park and ride for people travelling into the centre of Glasgow. The station complies with all recent accessibility legislation by having a footbridge served by both steps and lifts and platform access from the car parks available by both steps and ramps.

In early 2016, there were still a few of the Class 318 EMUs to be seen wearing the former Strathclyde crimson and cream colours but that livery did not last for long as the units were steadily being overhauled by Wabtec at Doncaster. After the mechanical and electrical work was completed, the sets were repainted into ScotRail's Saltire livery before being returned north.

Several images show some of the diverted services and engineering work that was carried out as part of the Edinburgh Glasgow Improvement Programme (EGIP). In order to carry out the required work at Queen Street, in Queen Street tunnel and on Cowlairs bank and to the junctions at Cowlairs, train services were diverted to start/stop at Queen Street Low Level, running there via Springburn and Anniesland. This made for some interesting photographic opportunities while the work was being undertaken but equally showed how the rail network could adapt to the line closure but keep essential services running.

One other event that applies to all the areas covered in this book was the restrictions that had to be imposed as a result of the Coronavirus pandemic in 2020. A good example as to how things had to be done differently was with the Railhead Treatment Train services (RHTT) that run during the leaf-fall period to keep the railhead surfaces clean. Normally, this would be done by an MPV (Multi-Purpose Vehicle) but in order to maintain the new requirements of social distancing, the 2020 season saw the use of a locomotive-hauled set of tanks with a Class 67 at each end. By fitting the outer end of each locomotive with a camera and placing a screen and controls in the inner cabs, the spray operative could see and work the railhead cleaning process without having to be in contact with the locomotive's driver.

Right: 334013 is seen jacked up inside Shields Road depot on 11 December 2016 undergoing maintenance before being reunited with its bogies, which were also having work done to them.

Below: 385102 was about to be unveiled to the media at Shields Road depot on 11 December 2016. The brand new Hitachi-built Class 385 EMU was not in service as it still had to undergo line testing and it was totally devoid of any interior fittings.

Exactly one month later on 11 January 2017, 385102 was occupying platform 2 at Gourock with many computers visible inside as it was undergoing night testing in that part of the world. It had been towed back to Gourock after the previous night's outing by 66115, which can be seen at the buffers. 314201 was about to depart with a ScotRail service to Glasgow Central.

380001 runs towards Shields Junction on the centre track at Cardonald on 29 September 2020 with the 10.36 Ardrossan Harbour to Glasgow Central. In the distance on the left, it's just possible to make out 385012, which was working the 11.06 Glasgow Central to Gourock while on the right-hand side, 385002 is visible as it approaches Hillington East with the 10.38 from Gourock to Glasgow Central.

156514 and 156504 wait at East Kilbride on 1 October 2020 with the 14.28 to Glasgow Central. The East Kilbride line is to be electrified in the near future so scenes like this with the Class 156s that have worked the line for many years will soon be history.

320414 arrives at Milngavie on 19 June 2020 with the 14.33 from Larkhall. The platforms at Milngavie have just been extended to hold nine coaches, which involved bringing the existing platform ends back into use and then extending the platforms further with associated alterations to the track, signalling and overheads.

334014 and 334011 arrive at Airdrie on 25 June 2020 with the 09.55 from Helensburgh Central to Edinburgh Waverley. All the services between Airdrie and Edinburgh are worked by Class 334 EMUs.

With 67020 leading and 67012 on the rear, the 12.55 Shettleston Loop to Slateford Yard Railhead Treatment Train is approaching Airdrie where, after using the crossover, it will reverse and return to Shettleston. This service has been worked by an MPV unit over the last few years but has reverted to being locomotive-hauled due to the Covid-19 pandemic in order to maintain social distancing between the driver and the spray operator.

Snow blankets the distant Campsie Fells as 68006 passes Greenfoot on 15 February 2016 with empty stock from a morning Fife rush-hour working to Edinburgh on its way to Motherwell for servicing.

In early 2016, there were still a few Class 318 EMUs in the former SPT crimson and cream livery to be seen. On 11 February 2016, 318265 runs past Greenfoot with a ScotRail service from Cumbernauld to Dalmuir.

A new station was built at Robroyston, between Springburn and Stepps in the outer Glasgow suburbs, and was opened on 15 December 2019, which was a very dull and wet day. On the much brighter 27 February 2020, 385103 arrives at Robroyston with the 10.25 from Glasgow Queen Street to Edinburgh Waverley via Cumbernauld and Falkirk Grahamston.

37685 passes Crowwood Grange on 29 June 2018 with a rake of coaches from Carnforth on their way to Fort William for use on the steam-hauled Jacobite tourist train.

GBRf ran a special charter for staff using the *Royal Scotsman* coaches and hauled by 66779 in its special green livery from Edinburgh Waverley to Rannoch and back on 13 October 2016. 66779 *Evening Star*, so named as it was the last Class 66 to be built, passes Crowwood Grange on its outward journey to Rannoch.

Running many hours late due to problems at Fort William, 37601 and 37612 pass Gartcosh on 3 October 2016 at 19.52 on their way to Exeter, which was not reached until well into the morning of the following day instead of what should have been a late evening arrival the same day.

The 14.10 departure from Freightliner's Coatbridge terminal to Crewe Basford Hall passes through Coatbridge Central on 17 February 2019 behind 90016 and 90047.

A Caledonian Sleeper trial run, with the new CAF Mark 5 coaches that had been built in Spain, from Fort William to Polmadie depot runs through Coatbridge Central on 9 March 2019 behind rebuilt 73970.

During the closure of Queen Street High Level for electrification work, the Edinburgh Waverley to Glasgow Queen Street express services were diverted to use Queen Street Low Level, running in via Anniesland and back to Edinburgh via Springburn. On 20 March 2016, 170471 and 170412 pass through Springburn on their way to Edinburgh with the 14.52 from Queen Street LL.

On their way to Queen Street Low Level, 170393 and 170460 approach Cowlairs North Junction with the 13.15 from Edinburgh Waverley on 9 May 2016 while 145446 waits to follow with a Falkirk Grahamston to Anniesland service.

156433 has just departed from Ashfield on 9 May 2016 with an Anniesland to Springburn working; another service that was introduced during the closure of Queen Street.

Just prior to Queen Street High Level closing for the electrification work, 170409 on the 12.30 to Edinburgh Waverley and 170414, in its special Borders Line livery with the 12.33 empty stock to Eastfield depot, are seen waiting at Queen Street.

As well as work at Queen Street and in Queen Street Tunnel, alterations were also carried out during the closure on Cowlairs Bank and at Cowlairs South Junction. This shows the scene at Cowlairs South Junction on 3 April 2016 with the main lines curving off to the left and the single track bi-directional line to and from Springburn on the right-hand side of the photograph.

Chapter 3
Lines Around Edinburgh

Dunbar on the East Coast Main Line originally had two platforms on loop lines through the station with the main lines bypassing the station to the south. The original down platform was demolished many years ago and the track lifted so that all trains that called at Dunbar used the one platform, which had been signalled for bi-directional working. Dunbar was, at that time, one of only two stations within Scotland not served by ScotRail, the other being Lockerbie.

As the population of Dunbar and its surrounding area increased with the building of hundreds of new houses, ScotRail started to run services from Edinburgh to Dunbar but to further increase the frequency of trains calling at Dunbar, it was obvious that another platform was required. A new down platform was built alongside the down main line and connected to the original station and platform by a new footbridge with the now usual arrangements of steps and lifts. A new station is planned to be constructed on the ECML at East Linton, again to meet the needs of people wanting to travel to and from Edinburgh for both work and leisure and, like Dunbar, to cater for an increased population as East Lothian is now a prime commuting area for those working in the city of Edinburgh.

Once again, new trains feature prominently in the changes that have occurred during this five-year period. LNER took over the running of passenger services that previously had been worked by Virgin Trains East Coast, and by the end of 2019, the HSTs that had worked services between London, Edinburgh and onwards to Inverness and Aberdeen had been replaced by a mix of all-electric and bi-mode Hitachi Azumas. The Class 91 electric locomotives that had worked in push-pull mode with sets of Mark 4 coaches were also displaced from the northern half of the ECML, being confined to a small number of services between London and either York or Leeds.

TransPennine Express started to operate a completely new service that used the northern half of the ECML running between Edinburgh Waverley and Liverpool Lime Street and like LNER, using a small fleet of five-car bi-mode Hitachi units similar to the LNER Azumas.

ScotRail was able to introduce some of its new Class 385 EMUs onto the services between Edinburgh and North Berwick, although the occasional service can still be worked by one of the older Class 380 EMUs. Diesel services on the Borders Line are a mix of Class 158s with an increasing number of services being worked by Class 170s. Pictured in this chapter, 170416 was one of a small batch that left ScotRail, being transferred to the new East Midlands Railway franchise and after an overhaul, it had worked its last couple of years with ScotRail in a plain blue livery instead of the usual Saltire colours.

As well as its new trains on the ECML, TransPennine Express also introduced the new Class 397 EMUs, which use Waverley station by running into Edinburgh on the line from Carstairs, as do Caledonian Sleeper with its Class 92 locos and Mark 5 Sleeper stock.

Two new platforms were constructed at Edinburgh Waverley, platforms 5 and 6, which were built long enough to accommodate the new Azumas. It is ironic to think that there were originally platforms in this position but they had become redundant in the 1960s when a lot of local services were withdrawn, later being filled in and converted to a car park. On security grounds, road vehicles ceased to use this area and so two new platforms were duly constructed.

A station that had undergone major work was Dunbar, where a second platform was constructed on the down main line. To link this with the existing platform and to make access easy for anyone with a disability, the new platform was joined to the existing one by a new footbridge with steps and lifts. The new platform is seen under construction on 13 August 2019 as 43299 and 43319 pass with the 11.46 from Newark North Gate to Edinburgh Waverley as 385039 and 385046 wait at the then single platform with the 15.12 service to Edinburgh Waverley.

The new platform was opened in December 2019 and on 17 December, 800113 is seen passing Dunbar on the up main line with the 09.52 from Aberdeen to King's Cross while 385044 and 385021 wait to depart at 13.01 to Edinburgh Waverley.

221134 passes East Linton, where a new station is to be built, on 26 August 2016 with a CrossCountry service from Glasgow Central to Penzance. Work on the new station should begin in 2021.

The new Hitachi Class 385 EMUs started to work services between Edinburgh Waverley and North Berwick on 12 September 2018 and on that date, 385007 and 385006 are seen arriving at North Berwick with the 10.43 from Edinburgh.

380103 approaches Drem Junction on 22 February 2017 with the 11.27 from North Berwick to Edinburgh Waverley.

91110 in its unique Royal Air Force Battle of Britain Memorial Flight livery approaches Drem on 16 February 2018 with the 09.00 from King's Cross to Edinburgh Waverley. The emblem on the locomotive's front depicts a Lancaster bomber with a Hurricane and a Spitfire fighter aircraft.

800201 in its all-over white hurries south through Drem on 12 September 2018 with a test working from Edinburgh Waverley to Doncaster.

With 43300 leading in its Craigentinny 100 livery, complete with the Golden Spanner emblem under the cab window, and with power car 43295 on the rear, the 09.52 from Aberdeen to London King's Cross thunders through Drem on 19 May 2018.

91115 speeds past Ballencrieff, between Drem and Longniddry, on 7 February 2020 with the 06.15 from King's Cross to Edinburgh Waverley.

A close-up of 91111 *For the Fallen* wearing what I consider to be the best special livery ever applied to a locomotive.

802212, a TransPennine bi-mode Hitachi IEP, passes Ballencrieff on 7 February 2020 with the 06.24 from Liverpool Lime Street to Edinburgh Waverley.

A pair of five-car LNER Azumas with 800202 leading 800208 pass Ballencrieff on 19 January 2020 with the 09.15 Newcastle to Edinburgh Waverley.

Bi-mode Azuma 800101 approaches Prestonpans in its very short-lived Virgin livery with an 08.36 Doncaster to Edinburgh Waverley test run. Virgin East Coast pulled out of running the franchise in June 2018, the service being run by the government's LNER operation since then.

158739 is seen at Gorebridge on the Borders line on 17 June 2017 with the 15.03 from Tweedbank to Edinburgh Waverley.

158709 has just departed from Newtongrange and is passing the former Lady Victoria Colliery, now the Scottish Mining Museum, on 17 June 2017 with the 15.26 from Edinburgh Waverley to Tweedbank.

170416 in plain-blue livery arrives at Newtongrange on 25 August 2019 with the 15.45 from Tweedbank to Edinburgh Waverley.

Platforms 5 and 6 under construction at Edinburgh Waverley on 11 December 2017.

91107 arrives at Edinburgh Waverley on 21 June 2018 with empty stock from Craigentinny that will shortly form a service to London King's Cross.

91107 arrives at the newly opened Platform 5 at Edinburgh Waverley on 13 March 2019 with the 09.00 LNER service from King's Cross.

Azuma 800106 is ready to depart from Platform 5 at Edinburgh Waverley on 18 June 2019 with the 14.48 training run to Newcastle. In platform 6, 220011 is just starting its engines and will shortly be working the 15.08 CrossCountry service to Plymouth.

43290 leads the 09.52 from Aberdeen to London King's Cross out of Edinburgh Waverley on 29 March 2018 with 43367 as the trailing power car.

800103 arrives at Edinburgh Waverley on 28 March 2019 on a training run from Newcastle.

66733 leaves Waverley on the short journey to Craigentinny depot with the empty *Royal Scotsman* coaches for servicing on 23 September 2016.

Preserved Class 50s 50007 and 50049, now sporting GBRf livery, pass through Kirknewton on 7 July 2019 with a 10.05 from Motherwell to Birmingham New Street charter.

92010 crosses Slateford Viaduct on 30 September 2017 with the old style Caledonian Sleeper empty stock from the overnight service from London Euston on its way to Polmadie depot in Glasgow for servicing.

92038 speeds across Slateford Viaduct on 6 July 2019 with a train made up of the new CAF-built Mark 5 sleeper stock, this being the overnight service from London Euston to Edinburgh Waverley.

A colourful sight! Due to a shortage of power cars, LNER had hired 43061, which is still in the colours of the former East Midlands Trains, from East Midlands Railway, and it is seen leading the 06.10 from Doncaster to Edinburgh Waverley as it crosses Slateford Viaduct on 30 September 2017. This had been diverted from Newcastle via the Tyne Valley line and then the WCML because of engineering work on the ECML between Newcastle and Edinburgh.

66712 starts to cross Slateford Viaduct on 30 September 2017 with a train of replaced track panels from Grantshouse to Carlisle New Yard.

Chapter 4
Edinburgh to the Forth Bridge and Fife

On the outskirts of Edinburgh on the line to the Forth Bridge is the relatively new station of Edinburgh Gateway, which was opened on 11 December 2016. It is a large staffed station with platforms long enough to accommodate an LNER Azuma and is linked to platforms at a lower level on the Edinburgh Trams line from Edinburgh Airport to York Place. Its usage has only been a small percentage of what was originally estimated due to the scaling back of the EGIP project.

The original plan was to divert two trains an hour between Edinburgh Waverley and Glasgow Queen Street in each direction to run via Edinburgh Gateway and provide a new chord between the line to the Forth Bridge and the Dalmeny Junction to Winchburgh Junction line, the latter of which would also be remodelled. However, the EGIP project was scaled back to save money with construction of the Dalmeny Chord abandoned along with the electrification of these lines.

In the original plans, Edinburgh Gateway was also going to be served by trains between Edinburgh, Fife and places further north, and also by trains coming north on the ECML and by passengers from the north of England, the Borders and by stations between Edinburgh and both Aberdeen and Inverness. Traffic from Edinburgh to Glasgow was estimated to account for the bulk of its intended usage but sadly that has not yet happened; the inter-city services between the north of England and Aberdeen have never called at Edinburgh Gateway so currently there is a large station with less than half the traffic that it was designed to accommodate.

As part of its plans to run the ScotRail franchise, Abellio had decided to use shortened HSTs with refurbished coaches that would also, amongst other improvements, have conductor-operated sliding doors. The HSTs came from Great Western Railway where they had been replaced by Hitachi IEP trains but as the delivery programme of these had ran late, the HSTs for ScotRail also arrived late.

The HSTs were to replace Class 170 Turbostars on most of ScotRail's longer distance services and as some Class 170s were due to move to other franchises in England, ScotRail obtained permission to temporarily run some HSTs in service using unrefurbished slam-door coaches. ScotRail classed these sets as 'Classic', which is why HSTs were seen with ScotRail painted power cars and either Great Western blue, green or a mix of both coloured coaches.

DRS provided Class 68s and Mark 2 coaches for the two morning and evening locomotive-hauled commuter services between Edinburgh and Fife. These workings initially had Saltire-liveried coaches and there were two Class 68s, 68006 and 68007, that also wore the Scotrail Saltire livery. When defects appeared in these coaches, DRS replaced them with their Mark 2 coaches. These were also fitted with retention toilet tanks, and whenever either 68006 or 68007 were unavailable, other Class 68s put in an appearance, which added to the variety of things to be photographed.

The LNER HSTs were phased out on the Aberdeen services, being replaced by the Hitachi bi-mode Azumas. A further change to workings in West Fife was that the *Royal Scotsman* luxury train, now usually hauled by a GBRf Class 66 in *Royal Scotsman* maroon livery, started to run on the much more scenic coast line between Inverkeithing and Thornton instead of via Dunfermline and Cowdenbeath.

I have used three images to illustrate another often overlooked fact. The HSTs were built between 1975 and 1982 and the majority of the Class 66s were constructed between 1998 and 2008, with 66746 being built in 2003. The A1 Pacific *Tornado* is a modern replica that was built in stages between 1994 and 2008, although it did not enter service until 2009, making it the newest of the three.

After the LNER HSTs had been withdrawn from everyday service, a set was repainted into the colours that the HSTs wore when they were first delivered to BR and a farewell tour was run in Scotland over two days. It went from Edinburgh to Inverness via Aberdeen on 18 December 2019 and then back to Edinburgh on 19 December before running south the following day on the ECML. I was fortunately able to photograph it on its way to Aberdeen in some glorious early morning light. At least in Scotland there are still the ScotRail HSTs to be seen in traffic!

170406 on the 11.07 from Edinburgh Waverley to Glenrothes with Thornton passes 158706 working the 10.27 from Glenrothes with Thornton to Edinburgh Waverley at the then not-long-opened Edinburgh Gateway station.

On 30 November 2019, 800108 runs off the Forth Bridge and passes through Dalmeny with the 09.52 Aberdeen to London King's Cross.

With 43179 leading and 43126 trailing, the 07.29 Dundee to Edinburgh ScotRail driver training extra leaves the Forth Bridge and approaches Dalmeny on 30 April 2018.

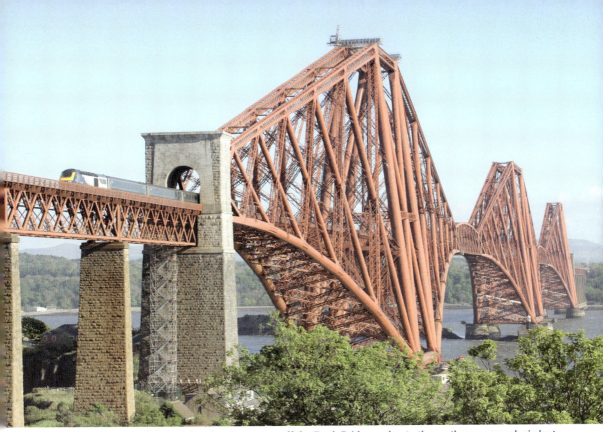

43021 leads the 17.39 from Edinburgh to Inverness off the Forth Bridge and onto the northern approach viaduct on 16 May 2019. 43026 was the rear power car and this was one of the 'Classic' sets that ran for a short while with GWR green coaches.

57306 passes North Queensferry on 6 May 2017 with the 06.30 Darlington to Dundee 'Northern Belle'.

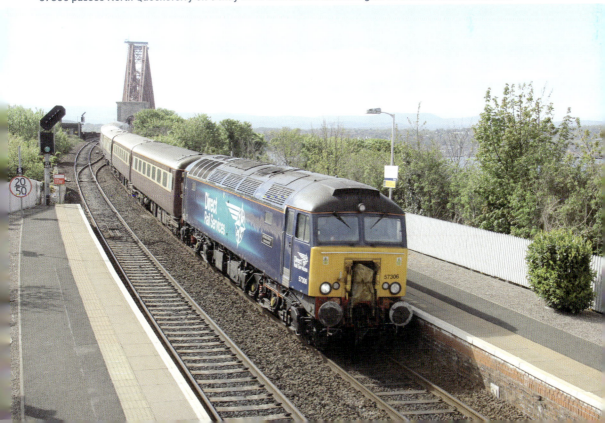

GBRf's BR large logo-liveried 66789 emerges from North Queensferry tunnel and passes through the station of the same name with a 09.15 Arbroath to Millerhill spoil working on 4 August 2019.

68017 powers upgrade from Inverkeithing to the Forth Bridge at Jamestown on 10 April 2017 with the 07.44 Glenrothes with Thornton to Edinburgh Waverley rush-hour locomotive-hauled service.

The National Railway Museum-liveried HST power car 43238 leads the 11.47 Aberdeen to King's Cross Virgin East Coast service at Jamestown on 6 November 2016 with 43257 on the rear.

The HSTs had all been removed from service on the ECML workings by the end of 2019, being replaced by the Hitachi-built Azumas. 800112 passes Jamestown on 23 July 2020 with the 14.52 from Aberdeen to King's Cross.

Diverted because of engineering work, 66423 brings the 10.00 Inverness to Mossend Stobart/Tesco service past Jamestown on 6 November 2016 on its way to the Forth Bridge.

170433 working the 17.09 from Aberdeen to Edinburgh Waverley passes 68033 in the up passenger loop at Inverkeithing East Junction with the 18.24 Cardenden to Mossend empty coaching stock on 27 June 2018.

In the last few days that the HSTs were working the LNER services to and from Aberdeen, the 07.08 Leeds to Aberdeen is seen at it passes the village of Hillend on its climb up from Inverkeithlng to Dalgety Summit on 30 November 2019 with 43290 leading and 43208 on the rear.

A1 Class 60163 *Tornado* climbs Dalgety Bank at Hillend on 14 March 2019 with the 10.14 Edinburgh Waverley to Aberdeen 'The Aberdonian'. It is strange to think that this locomotive, completed in 2008, is considerably newer than either the HST in the preceding image or the Class 66 in the following image.

The Belmond luxury touring train the *Royal Scotsman* passes Donibristle while climbing Dalgety Bank on 15 July 2019 with an Edinburgh to Aviemore Speyside working with 66746 providing the power.

68007 rolls into Aberdour on 1 June 2016 with the 18.23 from Glenrothes with Thornton to Edinburgh Waverley.

To commemorate the end of HST services on the ECML, LNER turned out a set in its original livery to work a final farewell tour. On its way from Edinburgh to Inverness via Aberdeen on 18 December 2019, the leading power car, 43312, was renumbered to its original number of 43112 and given its original set number of 254029 on the front. The repainted set is seen passing Pettycur, with Burntisland in the distance, as it approaches Kinghorn on its way north.

221139 passes Kinghorn on 3 May 2016 with the 08.20 Aberdeen to Penzance CrossCountry service.

Plain blue 170416 passes through Glenrothes with Thornton on 19 March 2017 with the 13.30 from Inverness to Edinburgh Waverley. In the distance, 158721 and 170475 wait to follow with the 16.20 Fife Circle service to Edinburgh Waverley.

73969, with 73971 on the rear, climbs up through Dunfermline Town on 10 April 2019 with a Caledonian Sleeper media special on its way to Townhill loop. Here, it would reverse and then head for Glasgow Central, where it had started earlier in the day.

68004 runs along the sea wall at Culross on 6 December 2020 with the diverted 10.47 Grangemouth to Aberdeen Craiginches intermodal, which ran to Perth via Dunfermline, Thornton, Ladybank and Newburgh to regain its normal route at Hilton Junction, south of Perth.

66555 passes Kincardine in glorious light on 19 April 2016 with a train of flyash from Aberthaw to Longannet to be used in manufacturing breeze blocks for the building trade.

Chapter 5

Edinburgh Waverley to Glasgow Queen Street via Falkirk High

In order to run the proposed timetable using eight-car Class 385 EMUs on a 15-minute frequency, it was obvious that some additional platform capacity would be required at Edinburgh Waverley. The solution was to demolish a building that had stood behind the buffers on what was a short platform 12, and lengthen that platform so that it could accommodate an eight-car train (two four-car Class 385/1s).

The Edinburgh Glasgow Improvement Programme should have seen the electric service running by 2017 but this plan did not go smoothly. The services were to have been worked by the new Hitachi Class 385 EMUs, which were late being delivered. Once the first few had arrived and were being tested, a fault was found that should never have arisen. The windscreen in front of the driver had curved glass but when running during the hours of darkness or in tunnels, the windscreen caused reflections that made accurate reading of signals difficult, leading to obvious safety concerns.

These two problems, and the associated delays in rectifying them, resulted in the initial electric services having to be worked by Class 380s borrowed from their normal use on Ayrshire services. A short-term solution was that ScotRail managed to acquire some Class 365 Networker EMUs that had recently been made surplus from duties in the outer London suburbs by the delivery of the new Class 700 EMUs. The air conditioning grille on the cab fronts of these trains made the Class 365s look as if they were smiling so ScotRail called them the 'Happy Trains' and their introduction enabled services between Edinburgh and Glasgow via Falkirk High to be operated by EMUs until the rectified Class 385s could be introduced.

The EGIP work unfortunately overran in both time and budget. When the work had started and some bridges had been rebuilt to enable clearance for the overhead wires, the European Union changed the regulations for new construction with the result that some of the bridge parapets that had been completed had to be raised, and work still to be done had to be redesigned. Additional clearances had to be made and this substantially increased the cost and time needed to complete the work.

As a flagship project, this issue, coupled with the media reaction to the curved windscreens on the Class 385s, resulted in the whole project unfortunately receiving some very negative press. The good news was that once the work was completed, and after the Class 385s entered service, the public were very quick to appreciate the improvements that had been made and this was reflected in the numbers of people who started to use the enhanced services.

All seemed to be going well and then 2020 arrived and the Edinburgh to Glasgow line was hit with two major problems. The Covid-19 pandemic saw passenger numbers fall away with many regular commuters being told to work from home and others finding that their work no longer even existed. Service frequency was reduced and then along came the storm in the early hours of 12 August 2020.

Scotland was battered by this intense event with thunder, incessant lightning and a torrential deluge of rain that caused almost instant flooding at numerous locations.

From Polmont to near Bo'ness Junction, the Union Canal runs almost parallel to the railway but at a slightly higher elevation to the south. During the storm, water flooded off the hillside to the south at the east side of Lathallan and poured into the canal. A long section of the northern canal bank collapsed and millions of gallons of water poured out of this breach, ran down and onto the railway line, flooding the lines, uprooting trees, scouring out ballast and supports for the overhead power lines and washing trees and soil onto the line. The problem was made worse as the Union Canal had been designed by Thomas Telford as a contour canal to eliminate locks, which slowed down canal traffic. With no locks for many miles, this simply resulted in an even greater amount of water pouring onto the line. One of the images that follows shows the main line at midday on 12 August and with all the damage that had been done, it meant that the line was completely closed for about six weeks for repair with two kilometres of line having to be completely rebuilt.

After all the work that had gone into upgrading the line, a fleet of new trains and Glasgow Queen Street having platforms lengthened and a new concourse built, the Covid-19 pandemic saw a reduction in both train frequency and a massive drop in the number of passengers using the services. With different working practices having been adopted by so many companies, how the future for Scotland's flagship route will be is a question that only time can answer.

The newly lengthened and commissioned platform 12 at Edinburgh Waverley is being used by 334037, which has just arrived from Helensburgh Central on 11 December 2017 as Virgin East Coast's 91128 departing with the 11.30 to London King's Cross.

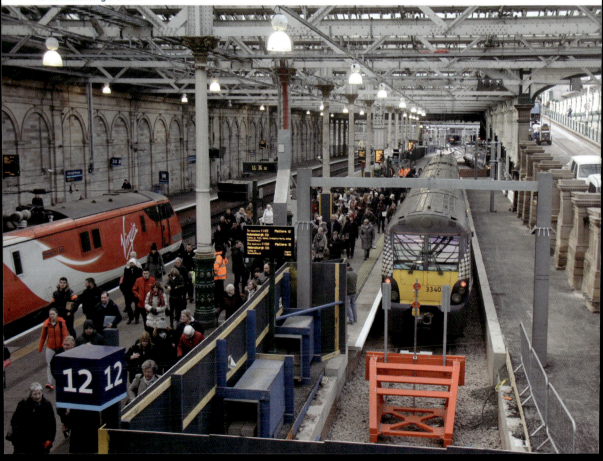

Edinburgh Waverley's west end on 18 June 2019 with 170396 on the 15.36 to Perth, 385115 on the 15.35 to Queen Street via Falkirk Grahamston and Cumbernauld, 43026 and 43031 on the 15.28 to Aberdeen and 385007 and 385122 on the 15.30 to Queen Street via Falkirk High.

Haymarket looking east on 3 August 2017 with 334002 and 334009 working the 15.50 from Waverley to Helensburgh Central as 390103 arrives with the 15.52 from Waverley to London Euston.

Looking west from Haymarket on 15 October 2018; 334009 is on the 11.37 Waverley to Milngavie as 334003 approaches with the 09.56 from Helensburgh Central while on the Fife lines, 158734 is on the 11.37 from Edinburgh Waverly to Perth as 170425 approaches Haymarket with the 10.53 from Glenrothes with Thornton.

With Arthur's Seat and the Salisbury Crags prominent in the distance, 334018 and 334031 approach Edinburgh Park on 7 February 2019 with the 13.10 from Waverley to Milngavie.

67007 runs along the E&G at Park Farm, just to the east of Linlithgow, on 2 January 2019 with a 10.11 Polmadie to Inverness sleeper empty stock move.

Sometimes you get very lucky, as in this case. I was waiting to photograph the northbound King's Cross to Inverness HST at Park Farm on 19 April 2016 when I heard a Class 68 approaching from the west and I managed to get both the HST and the DRS Class 68 on a heavily delayed Motherwell to Edinburgh empty stock (running over an hour late) in the picture. 68020 and 43314 therefore made a unique photograph, only possible by my being in the right place at exactly the right time.

Every four weeks, the New Measurement Train HST is scheduled to work a 10.38 Heaton depot (Newcastle) to Newcastle via Glasgow Queen Street test run. On 29 January 2018, at Park Farm 43062 leads with 43013 on the rear as it speeds towards Glasgow.

There has always been the occasional unusual working and this was definitely one such example. On 25 July 2016, 20205 and 20189 hauled prototype HST power car 41001 and its three matching Mark 3 coaches on an 08.47 Bo'ness Junction to York Holgate after visiting the Bo'ness and Kinneil Railway.

An event that had to be recorded. On 9 December 2019, 43296 and 43239 pass Park Farm with the very last HST-worked 07.55 Inverness to King's Cross 'Highland Chieftain'. From the following day, the Inverness to King's Cross LNER service went over to being fully worked by the Azuma bi-mode units.

Due to delays to deliveries of the new Hitachi-built Class 385 EMUs, ScotRail managed to obtain a short-term hire of some redundant Networker Class 365 EMUs that had previously been working out of King's Cross. Called 'Happy Trains' by ScotRail, 365525 and 365509 pass Park Farm on 27 June 2018 with the 15.30 from Edinburgh Waverley to Glasgow Queen Street.

On Sunday 24 June 2018, the E&G was closed east of Linlithgow for engineering work and this shows 380017 and 380104 after arriving at Linlithgow from Queen Street. While the passengers had to complete their journey to Edinburgh using buses, the two Class 380s crossed over before working the next service back to Queen Street.

Another unexpected sight was the use of Caledonian Sleeper-liveried Class 86/4 86401 on a Scottish Railway Preservation Society railtour between Waverley and Queen Street on 1 June 2018. 86401 is seen passing through Linlithgow at speed with 37025 on the rear.

LNER Azuma 800101 crosses Linlithgow Viaduct on 8 August 2020 with the 12.00 King's Cross to Inverness 'Highland Chieftain'.

Substituting for the usual NMT yellow HST, 67027, with 67023 on the rear, passes Lathallan on 27 March 2017 with the 10.38 Heaton depot to Newcastle on its way back from Glasgow Queen Street.

DRS used to send the stock that would work the two evening locomotive-hauled services from Edinburgh Waverley to Fife from Motherwell depot to Edinburgh by two routes. One worked via the Shotts line and the other via the E&G. On 31 August 2017, 68032 passes Lathallan with the empty stock from Motherwell to Edinburgh Waverley.

Scotland was battered by an intense thunderstorm with torrential rain in the early hours of 12 August 2020. This caused widespread damage, most notably the crash of a HST between Carmont and Stonehaven and the flooding of the E&G just to the east of Lathallan due to the northern bank of the Union Canal collapsing. This shows part of the damage at Lathallan late in the morning of 12 August that resulted in the line being closed for a month and a half.

365513 arrives at Polmont on 16 May 2018 on an Eastfield depot to Linlithgow loop crew training run.

To afford adequate clearance for the overhead power cables, the trackbed through Falkirk High Tunnel was lowered and the old line replaced by concrete slab track, which can be seen in this photograph as 385041 leading the 12.45 from Waverley to Queen Street emerges from the tunnel on 13 August 2019.

385019 leads the 12.30 Glasgow Queen Street to Edinburgh Waverley into Falkirk High on 13 March 2019.

There have been occasions when the NMT HST has been unavailable so a set of test coaches with a locomotive at each end has substituted. On 12 September 2016, the 10.38 Heaton to Newcastle via Glasgow Queen Street passes Greenhill Upper Junction with 68018 leading to Queen Street and with 68005 on the rear, which would take the train back south from Queen Street to Newcastle. By this date, the masts for the forthcoming electrification were being erected.

Up until the electric services commenced, the services between Waverley and Queen Street had been worked by the Class 170 DMUs since their introduction. This shows 170427 and 170456 working the 13.00 from Queen Street to Waverley at Greenhill Upper Junction on 25 September 2016. As there was not sufficient clearance to place the masts on the south side of the lines beside the track, several masts had unusually to be built on the roadside of the railway boundary.

This was not an easy photograph to take; there was very little warning of the train approaching with an almost silent EMU and road traffic noise coupled with the train running at around the 90mph mark. However, I managed to catch 380104 crossing Castlecary Viaduct over the M80 motorway on 24 June 2018 with a Queen Street to Linlithgow shuttle; a shot only possible for a few days either side of the longest day.

66733 passed Breich on 18 July 2017 with the 06.25 North Blyth to Fort William alumina tanks. The old Breich station had low platforms, a very dilapidated footbridge and a wooden hut on the up side to Edinburgh that served as a rudimentary waiting shelter for the occasional passenger who used the only eastbound service that called there each weekday.

With the old station completely demolished, work on installing the infrastructure for the electrification was well under way when 66101 passed Breich on 3 July 2018, with a load of pipes from Hartlepool to Georgemas for use by the North Sea oil Industry.

Chapter 6

The Electrification of the Shotts Line

When the decision was made to electrify the Edinburgh to Glasgow line via Falkirk High and then to continue electrifying the lines via Falkirk Grahamston to Cumbernauld, Alloa and Dunblane, it was also decided to electrify the Shotts line. Despite claims by various sources that the line between Edinburgh and Glasgow via Shotts would be electrified, in actual fact it was only the central 23 miles that needed to see the wires go up. The line from Edinburgh Waverley to Midcalder Junction was already electrified, as was the line from Glasgow Central to Holytown Junction, which meant that the line could be completed relatively easily.

One major decision that had an effect on the cost of the work was the one to completely rebuild the station at Breich. It had been proposed for closure but this was rejected and so it was decided that a complete rebuild was required to bring it up to the required standards of both construction and passenger access, rather than try to upgrade the old station. The old station at Breich had low platforms and access to the Edinburgh-bound platform was via a very old and rather worn footbridge. As a result, the station did not meet the modern requirements of the accessibility legislation. Other stations along the line were all rebuilt to ensure passengers could easily access platforms by either steps or lifts unless there were other easy means, such as ramped access from adjacent roads.

The electrification work commenced in 2017 and was completed by the spring of 2019, this being finished on time and within its budget of £160 million. Test runs along the new line were made on 25 February 2019 using Freightliner's 86638, and electric units then started to appear on crew learning runs before certain electric services started on 23 April 2019. In the interim, the remaining services continued to be worked by either Class 156 or Class 158 DMUs.

When the next timetable change was made, a full electric service was introduced with most services operated by the new three-car Hitachi Class 385s but with one diagram using a Class 380. As with the entire network, some services on the line had been withdrawn by the end of 2020 as a result of the Covid-19 pandemic, so the frequency of services at certain times is now running at a reduced level.

Although the Class 156s were the mainstay of services on the Shotts line, there were an ever increasing number of Class 158s to be seen by the summer of 2017. On 18 July of that year, 158741, still in the old First Group colours, passes through Breich with a service from Glasgow Central to Edinburgh Waverley.

37099 leads the 'Mentor' test train out of Glasgow Queen Street on 14 December 2018 on its way to Edinburgh Waverley; being able to photograph a split-headcode box Class 37 at the terminus where they were once so common was a very pleasant surprise and one I never thought possible at the end of 2018.

The new image at Glasgow Queen Street as 385112 leads the 10.30 from Edinburgh Waverley into the station on 13 December 2018.

Two of the new Hitachi Class 385 EMUs pass at Croy on 4 February 2019, 385112 was the rear unit on the 14.00 from Queen Street to Waverley as 385109 arrived working the 13.41 from Alloa to Queen Street.

One of ScotRail's refurbished HST sets, with 43135 leading and 43037 trailing, thunders through Lenzie on 1 June 2020 working the 12.08 from Glasgow Queen Street to Inverness.

Fast forward to 17 September 2019 as 57314 went west with an Edinburgh to Auchinleck 'Northern Belle' with 57601 on the rear. Breich now has the correct height of platforms, modern lighting, a public address system, security cameras and a waiting shelter on each platform; transformation complete!

Another new intermodal flow started on 3 November 2020 when 66783 powered a Doncaster to Elderslie working, seen as it passes Breich.

380103 runs past Breich on 17 September 2019 with the 09.56 from Edinburgh Waverley to Glasgow Central. In the distance, 397002 was working a 10.05 Glasgow Central to Slateford test run.

Stations on the Shotts line were all rebuilt with step-free access to both platforms, either by easily accessed paths or by footbridges with both steps and lifts as can be seen in this view at West Calder on 18 September 2020 as 385011 arrives with the 14.27 from Edinburgh Waverley to Glasgow Central.

A busy scene at Shotts on 4 June 2019; 385022 on the left was working the 08.57 from Edinburgh Waverley to Glasgow Central while 385019 on the right was heading to Edinburgh Waverley with the 09.04 from Glasgow Central.

On 4 June 2019, 380103 has just arrived at Fauldhouse with the 08.17 from Glasgow Central to Edinburgh Waverley. Fauldhouse, like several other stations on the Shotts line, had had a new footbridge with lifts and steps installed to meet the requirements of disability legislation.

Chapter 7

Polmont to Cumbernauld via Falkirk Grahamston and the Grangemouth Branch

Afrer the main line electrification between Edinburgh Waverley and Glasgow Queen Street via Falkirk High had been completed, attention quickly turned to wiring the lines from Polmont to Falkirk Grahamston, the Grangemouth branch and on via Camelon and the Larbert triangle to Greenhill and then the final few miles to Cumbernauld. At Cumbernauld, it joined with the already electrified lines to Queen Street and Mossend. This also created the fifth electrified line between Glasgow and Edinburgh with a new service running half-hourly between Queen Street High Level and Edinburgh Waverley via Cumbernauld and Falkirk Grahamston. In the event of anything going wrong with the line through Falkirk High, services on that line can now be diverted to run from Greenhill Upper via Camelon and Falkirk Grahamston before rejoining the main line at Polmont Junction.

There was great political pressure to electrify the Grangemouth branch, a line that at present has no passenger service but is a main freight artery with fuel trains running from Grangemouth oil terminal and intermodal container traffic from a terminal at Fouldubs and from within Grangemouth Docks. Despite the line being wired in 2018, there is still no regular freight service that is electrically hauled and diesel power is still the norm on intermodal services between Grangemouth and Daventry. This is a service that runs virtually the entire distance under overhead wires but is not hauled by electric traction.

For many years, the problem for traffic in the docks has been the short length of the siding used for container traffic but, late in 2020, Forth Ports commenced work on extending the length of the siding and the run-round loop so that by early 2021, it will be able to accommodate trains that are the maximum length allowed on the national network. This development should also produce more train services running to and from the docks.

A further change to the local rail scene occurred when Colas Railfreight won the contract to operate the majority of the fuel trains running from Grangemouth oil terminal. Initially, Colas used a Class 60 on the evening train to Dalston in Cumbria but then surprised a lot of people by ordering a further nine Class 70s, which were constructed at Erie, Pennsylvania, from General Electric. After the new locomotives arrived, Colas then sold its ten Class 60s to GBRf. On lighter flows, it was also a surprise to see a return of Class 56 locomotives, a type that EWS had eliminated when it had taken delivery of its new Class 66s.

It has been all change on the passenger side with all of the ScotRail services running through Falkirk Grahamston now diagrammed to be worked by Class 385 EMUs and after early December 2019, the LNER HST service between London King's Cross and Inverness started to be worked by a Hitachi

Class 800 bi-mode, which enabled this service to now run on electric power between Edinburgh and just south of Dunblane, where the Azumas switch to diesel mode.

Network Rail uses a wide variety of track machines for various types of track maintenance and renewal. These are really the railways' unsung heroes, very often working at night or when a line is under the possession of engineers. One type sometimes seen more frequently are the Windhoff MPVs (Multi-Purpose Vehicles). One task that they were used on in Central Scotland each autumn was cleaning the railhead surfaces to enable accurate braking and help to avoid wheelflats, which are caused when brakes are applied and the wheel locks and slides along the rail.

The final image in this section shows one of several special trains that ScotRail organised on 18 December 2019 with the last pair of Class 314 EMUs to remain in service. I photographed 314202 and 314205 at Cumbernauld as they entered the station after using the turnback siding. Built in 1979, the class had given yeoman service over the years on various Glasgow suburban lines and their withdrawal was just another illustration of the tremendous change on the rail network in the five years covered in this book.

170470 arrives at Polmont on 9 August 2018 with the 13.03 from Edinburgh Waverley to Dunblane.

68017 is climbing upgrade from Falkirk Grahamston towards Polmont at Lauriston on 24 July 2017 with the empty stock from Motherwell to Edinburgh Waverley for an evening locomotive-hauled service to Fife.

66746 has 47739 behind it and then the SRPS railtour coaches, returning to Bo'ness from Newcastle on 2 May 2017.

43257 leads the southbound 'Highland Chieftain', the 07.55 Inverness to King's Cross, through the reverse curves at Lauriston on 3 May 2017.

56113 runs through Falkirk Grahamston with empty aviation fuel tanks from Prestwick returning to Grangemouth on 11 May 2016.

The 07.55 Inverness to King's Cross on 4 March 2020 was worked by 800103, photographed as it arrived at Falkirk Grahamston with a cheery wave to the photographer from the driver.

56302 is on the single line to Grangemouth oil terminal on 3 July 2017 with empty fuel tanks from Fort William. Once EWS had withdrawn all of its Class 56s, I do not suppose anyone ever thought that they would enjoy a second life in this part of the world with Colas Railfreight!

88001 worked the first Daventry to Grangemouth Docks intermodal and is on the single track line to Grangemouth Docks on 29 June 2019. Despite the Grangemouth branch being electrified, at the end of 2020 this remained the only electric locomotive to work into Grangemouth and, being a bi-mode, then able to work into the docks using its diesel engine.

The Saturdays-only Grangemouth to Daventry intermodal leaves the run-round loops at Fouldubs on 5 May 2017 behind a very clean 66044 that had recently been repainted into DB red.

Evening departures at Fouldubs Junction, Grangemouth. 60056 has just got the road and is starting the climb up to Grangemouth Junction with the Grangemouth Oil Terminal to Dalston loaded fuel train. Sitting in the run-round loop is 66003, which will shortly follow the Class 60 with the evening Grangemouth to Daventry intermodal on 3 July 2017.

68024 has just departed from Fouldubs on 4 May 2017 with the daily 12.24 Grangemouth to Aberdeen intermodal, seen passing the WH Malcolm warehouses.

66109 was painted into this special livery and named *Teesport Express*. It is often to be found working the 04.22 Tees Dock to Grangemouth intermodal and the return afternoon working back to Teesside. On 6 May 2020, it was nearing journey's end when it passed through Camelon with only a few more miles to go to its destination.

70805 is approaching Camelon on 5 April 2019 with the empty oil tanks from Dalston to Grangemouth oil terminal.

With 57316 leading and 57313 on the rear, the 17.02 returning railtour from Dundee to Whitehaven passes Greenhill Lower Junction on 8 June 2016.

Ten months after the West Coast Class 57s had passed Greenhill Lower Junction with the Dundee to Whitehaven railtour, the majority of the masts for the forthcoming electrification had been erected and what was once a great location for photographs was rapidly becoming one where it was more and more difficult to take a good photograph. 66118 passes Greenhill Lower on 5 April 2017 with the calcium carbonate tanks from Aberdeen Waterloo Quay to Mossend.

An opportunity that is only possible for a few weeks either side of Midsummer's day is being able to photograph the Grangemouth Oil Terminal to Dalston loaded tanks passing Allandale. On 19 June 2017, they are behind 70802 as the masts go up and another location is about to be lost.

Not often seen but real workhorses on the entire network are the Network Rail fleet of MPVs. This shows DR98911 and DR98961 passing Allandale on 1 December 2017 on railhead treatment duties; using high-pressure water jets to clean the rails and where it is required, spreading sandite onto the rails to improve adhesion and braking, principally for passenger services.

On the bitterly cold morning of 1 February 2019 after a severe overnight frost, 385109 passes Allandale with the 10.03 from Edinburgh Waverley to Glasgow Queen Street via Falkirk Grahamston and Cumbernauld. This is the fifth different electrified service that now links Scotland's two largest cities.

While work was being carried out on the line between Aberdeen and Inverurie, the Waterloo tanks had to run for a short while with a Class 66 at each end. On 21 June 2018, the train is seen as it approaches Cumbernauld with 66023 leading and 66015 on the rear. In the turnback siding, 320317 waits for the freight to pass before it can emerge and use the crossover before working a Cumbernauld to Dumbarton Central service.

18 December 2019 was a day when we said goodbye to two types of train. In the morning, in glorious winter sunshine, I had photographed the LNER HST that had been repainted into its original livery at Pettycur and then nearly five hours later in poor light and heavy rain, I photographed this ScotRail-organised special; a farewell to the Class 314 EMUs. The final train was made up of 314205 and 314202 and this shows the pair, still in their Strathclyde carmine and cream colours, leaving the turnback siding at Cumbernauld prior to embarking their passengers and returning to Glasgow Central.

The two rush-hour locomotive-hauled services between Edinburgh and Fife were withdrawn after the start of the COVID-19 pandemic lockdown restrictions. The second train from Edinburgh terminated at Cardenden and the empty stock then returned to Mossend via Falkirk Grahamston and Cumbernauld. On 21 June 2018, 68007 approaches Cumbernauld with the empty stock from Cardenden.

Chapter 8
Larbert to Perth and the Stirling to Alloa Line

The line from Larbert to Stirling and Dunblane, and the line from Stirling to Alloa, were electrified in 2018 along with some associated modifications to track and signalling. If the first stage of EGIP had taken longer to complete and cost more than was budgeted, this part of the network improvement was completed both within time and budget. As the Alloa line is single track from the outskirts of Stirling to Alloa with only one passing loop at Cambus, the decision was made to completely close the line for a few months while all the required work was carried out. This plan worked well and the benefits of having a much improved service was recognised by an increase in train usage with passenger numbers showing a steady increase.

Alas in early 2020, the Covid-19 pandemic arrived and this has had a huge impact on passenger services. With as many people as possible being told to work from home and others told not to travel, there was only a core of essential workers now using the various services. I have used two photos to try to illustrate the effects of the pandemic but what I have shown at my local station of Larbert could be echoed across the country at any other station; previously busy commuter services running with either hardly any passengers or even in some cases with no passengers at all.

Long distance travel was equally affected and the only positive note was that with fewer passenger services running, there was the potential for more freight trains to operate. If the government's position on climate change is to be taken seriously, then greater usage of the rail network with more emphasis on electrification and other low-emission methods would seem to be the way forward.

A good example of what can be achieved is the construction of the new rail freight facility at Blackford, Perthshire, which will be used by Highland Spring to take containers loaded with bottled water to its markets using rail. It took many years for this plan to arrive but it will generate more freight traffic and also reduce the number of lorries using the local roads. This idea could be done at many more places across the country and it is to be hoped that this will happen and that Blackford will not be an isolated example.

The Alloa line lost its coal traffic to Longannet when the power station closed in the early spring of 2016 but there are now plans for the construction of a factory there to build trains by the Spanish company Talgo. As part of that plan, work is now being carried out on upgrading the line beyond Alloa to Longannet with plans to extend electrification and to construct three new stations at Clackmannan, Kincardine and Longannet so it is hoped that all this will be realised.

The Covid-19 pandemic also had a huge impact on tourist and leisure businesses. Charter trains from the south and internal ones organised amongst others by the Scottish Railway Preservation Society (who use their own railtour coaches) were seen on a regular basis on most weekends along with the various tours of the luxury *Royal Scotsman* (the nearest thing to a five star hotel on wheels according to its train manager) but the vast majority of these ceased running. If it again becomes possible to run these excursions, it is thought that with so many people now working from home, the rail network could benefit from an upsurge in leisure travel. In the future, there are plans to extend the electrification from Dunblane to Perth, and will electrification stop there?

The 13.05 Inverness to Mossend intermodal approaches Plean Summit on 4 May 2017 with 68023 providing the power.

In its unique British Transport Police livery, 170407 passes Plean, where the masts were rapidly going up, on 14 July 2018 with the 16.33 from Edinburgh Waverley to Dunblane.

385124 waits at platform 6 at Stirling on 31 August 2019 with the 14.51 from Queen Street to Alloa. The original footbridge was raised in height to clear the overhead wires as it was a listed structure, and a new lift tower and steps were constructed so that platforms 9 and 10 were joined to the rest of the station and fully met the requirements of the Disability Discrimination Act.

Part of the electrification work involved track modifications and alterations to signalling. At Larbert, the two former down loops were replaced by one, and two new sidings for track machines were constructed on the up side. This shows work at Larbert on 5 November 2016 with 66170 in the distance at the head of an engineering train.

37405 with inspection saloon *Caroline* passes through Larbert on 9 August 2018, running as a 07.38 from Perth to Carlisle.

37605 and 37259 disturbed the rural sounds as they roared up the climb from Larbert to the summit at Plean on 14 April 2017 with a 05.12 Pathfinder railtour from Eastleigh to Inverness with a rapidly fading rainbow ending at Plane Castle in the near distance.

The station seats at Larbert had stickers fixed to them advising that some parts of the seat were not in use in order to maintain social distancing. This was a change forced on the rail network like no other; it was unprecedented.

There is a four-weekly test train that runs from Mossend to Inverness and during the time covered by this book, it has been powered by Class 37s supplied by Colas, then by DRS and finally, once again, by Colas. As Colas did not have enough Class 37s of its own, in some cases it hired and even purchased locomotives from preservation societies. On 9 July 2016, InterCity-liveried 37254 was leading with 37175 on the rear as the train went north through Larbert.

As elsewhere, the line between Larbert and Perth has seen a transformation with the introduction of new types of rolling stock and traction so it does enable me to finish this chapter on a positive note. The pandemic has caused chaos to so many lives and working habits but it will pass, it will take time but when one looks at the changes that have happened in such a short time, one can only pause and wonder what the future will hold for the railways of Central Scotland.

The five years covered by this book witnessed the electrification of the Edinburgh to Glasgow main line and then extensions to Dunblane and Alloa as well as the Shotts line. These events had a major influence in shaping the modern railway network and yet this work was totally undone by the Covid-19 pandemic of 2020. Trains had few passengers due to lockdown and this can be best illustrated by this photograph of 158707 and 158728 at Larbert on 15 May 2020. The train is the 17.09 from Queen Street to Dundee, first stop Larbert. Prior to the pandemic, some 60 or more passengers would have alighted and there would have been a line of cars waiting to collect some of them. The two Class 158s arrived and waited before heading off to their next stop at Stirling but no one got off, no one got on and apart from the driver and conductor, there was not one other person on board the four-coach train. On the other platform, there were no passengers waiting for the next train to Edinburgh, the station was just eerily quiet and empty.

385106 departs from Alloa on 1 September 2019 with the 15.16 to Glasgow Queen Street. Electric services to Alloa commenced in December 2018.

Freightliner's 66503 in the colours of Genesee and Wyoming, the new owner of Freightliner, hauls the medium output ballast train at Manor Powis on its way from Alloa to Millerhill on 18 June 2020.

Prior to electrification, 68001 runs through Dunblane station on 30 June 2018 with the 13.10 intermodal from Inverness to Mossend.

This was Dunblane after the wires had gone up and who would ever have imagined that the electric units that were initially to work the new services would be Class 365 Networkers displaced from their former duties around London. 365537 on the left had just arrived at Dunblane from Edinburgh while 365525 on the right was about to depart with the 12.28 to Edinburgh Waverley on 23 February 2019.

If seeing a pair of Networker EMUs at Dunblane was unusual then this photograph verges on the bizarre. For many years, the Class 73 electro-diesels were confined to their home area on the Southern Region and no one had ever dreamed that six would be rebuilt to haul sleeper services north of the Central Belt in Scotland. Nevertheless, this is what happened and on 23 February 2019 with 73970 leading and 73969 on the rear, the 10.02 Aberdeen to Polmadie depot passes through Dunblane. In the distance, 365537 is waiting to cross over and then work the 12.58 from Dunblane to Edinburgh Waverley.

Another illustration that shows the influence the Covid-19 pandemic has had on the rail network; 43033 leads an Aberdeen to Queen Street ScotRail express south at Greenloaning, between Blackford and Dunblane, with 43033 wearing a vinyl face mask to promote the wearing of such items while on public transport. 43181 was on the rear on 24 October 2020.

LNER Azuma 800113 speeds south past the new Blackford rail freight facility with the 07.55 from Inverness to King's Cross on 24 December 2020. The new facility should be ready to receive its first train towards the middle of 2021.

68003 approaches Blackford on 2 October 2020 with the 13.19 intermodal from Inverness to Mossend.

60047 passes Blackford on 27 October 2017 with the 05.55 Oxwellmains to Aberdeen cement. The consist has one new JPA bogie wagon behind the locomotive followed by a raft of the older four-wheeled PCAs.

The Sundays-only 09.10 from Edinburgh to Aberdeen was diverted north via Stirling and Perth to Dundee as its normal route over the Forth Bridge was closed for maintenance on 14 February 2016. With 43274 leading and 43313 trailing, the HST passes Blackford on a bitterly cold morning after overnight snow.

On 19 December 2018, 70811 and 70801 pass Bardrill with a late-running 05.55 cement from Oxwellmains to Aberdeen. 70801 had suffered a headlight failure so 70811 had rescued the delayed train from the loop at Drem and then took the train with 70801 to Aberdeen and back.

37610 rounds the curve at Bardrill on 22 September 2016 while taking Network Rail's Scottish Snow Train from Perth to Kilmarnock for repairs before it would be needed when winter arrives on the Highland Main Line. The leading wagon is used to clear frozen points using hot air blowers and steam lances.

68016 speeds north at Bardrill on 15 February 2016 with the 12.23 intermodal from Grangemouth to Aberdeen.

From a photography perspective, full sun with snow on the ground, a blue sky and a colourful train is a winning combination. On 15 February 2016, Colas Railfreight's 60076 runs north at Gleneagles with the 05.55 Oxwellmains to Aberdeen cement.

A fully refurbished ScotRail HST with 43136 leading and 43135 on the rear approaches Gleneagles on 8 August 2020 with the 08.41 from Glasgow Queen Street to Aberdeen.

Railtours from various places in England were regular happenings before the Covid-19 pandemic and normally played an important part in the Scottish tourist industry. On 23 May 2018, with 57316 leading and 47772 on the rear, the 15.41 Perth to York powers through Gleneagles at almost the top of the long climb up from Hilton Junction, just to the south of Perth.

170432 speeds downhill towards Perth at Forteviot on 18 January 2020 while working the 09.40 from Glasgow Queen Street to Aberdeen.

Caledonian Sleeper's 73971 passes Forteviot on 18 January 2020 with a 10.03 empty sleeper coaches movement from Aberdeen to Polmadie depot.

In BR green and carrying their original numbers, D6851 and D6817 (alias 37667 and 37521) pass Forteviot on 27 September 2020 with a 12.39 private charter from Perth to Darlington North Road.

This was one of the last services that I photographed with ex-GWR slam door Mark 3 coaches in their original livery, called an HST 'Classic' set by ScotRail. On 18 January 2020, with 43144 leading and 43030 on the rear, the 09.44 from Aberdeen to Glasgow Queen Street hurries past Forteviot.

This was the south end of Perth station on Sunday 12 January 2020 with 170451, which would work an early train the following morning from Markinch to Edinburgh Waverley, LNER's 800105 on the 09.40 from Inverness to King's Cross and finally 66733 and 73969 on sleeper coaches. The evening sleeper from Inverness was to start at Perth because when the Friday evening sleeper service from Euston to Inverness had tried to go north from Perth, it had encountered flooded track near Dunkeld and Birnam and so had returned to Perth; its passengers completed their journey by road.

Further reading from

As Europe's leading transport publisher, we produce a wide range of railway magazines and bookazines.